BOATS AND SHIPS

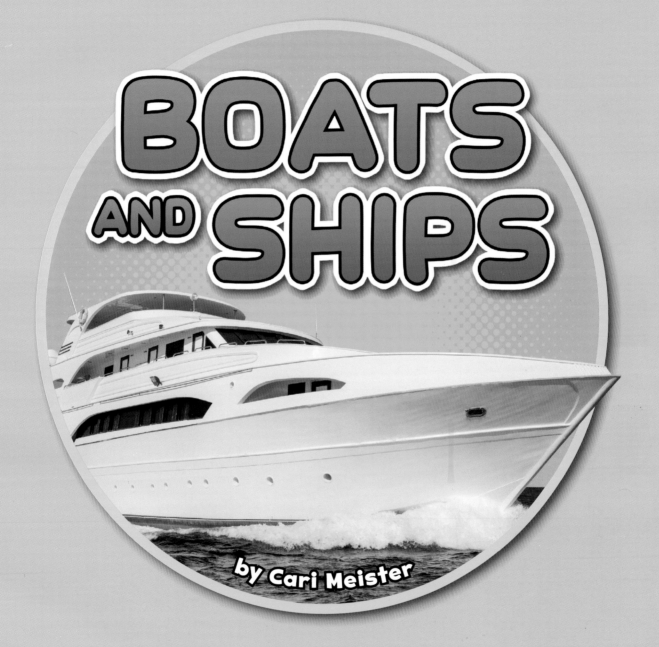

by Cari Meister

raintree

a Capstone company — publishers for children

Boats and ships take us to places! Ships are larger
than boats. Some boats are tiny, just for one
person. Some ships are huge, like floating hotels.
Different boats and ships do different jobs.

Boats and ships float in the water.

hull from underneath →

The main body of the boat is called the hull.

bow

The front of the boat is the bow.

stern

The back is the stern.

There are many types of boats
and ships.
Ferries are large ships. They carry
people and cars across the water.

Tugboats pull big ships in and out of harbours.

SPLISH!

SPLASH!

Canoes and kayaks are small boats.
They usually carry one or two people.
People use paddles to get these boats moving.

There goes a speedboat.
It races through the water.

Speedboats can be used to pull people along on skis. This is called waterskiing. It is a fun sport!

Sailing boats use wind to make them go. The wind catches the sails. It pushes the boat through the water. These sailing boats are racing!

WHOOOOSH!

Some ships are cabin cruisers. They have beds and living space inside. Some have kitchens too. They are like little holiday houses.

The cabin cruiser's hull is shaped like a big V.
It cuts smoothly through the water.

Yachts are big, fancy cabin
cruisers. People can use them
to explore the world.

Yachts are usually very expensive.
They are very comfortable. Some
even have hot tubs for relaxing in.

Icebreaker ships can move through water covered in ice. They cut through the ice. They make safe ways for other ships to travel through.

All aboard!

People take holidays on cruise ships.
These big ships often have pools, restaurants
and cinemas on board.

They sail to beautiful places.
Some cruise ships can carry
up to 5,000 people.

Cargo ships carry goods instead of
passengers. They travel across seas
and oceans.

A reefer ship is a refrigerated cargo ship.
It carries fruit, meats and other food.

Military ships are used by the navy.
They watch over the land and seas.

Military ships are sometimes used in wars. They can help people in need.

BLUB. BLUB. BLUB.

Submarines are ships that can go underwater. The navy uses submarines to watch out for enemy ships.

Scientists use smaller submarines to observe
sea animals. Submarines help people discover
new things under water.

Engineers are always thinking of new ideas.
They work to make boats faster and more powerful.

What kind of boat would you like to see in the future?

Timeline

1800s

Until the 1800s, most boats were made from wood. In the 1800s, iron and steel ships are introduced. Ships begin to be powered by steam instead of sails.

1900

1955

The first hovercraft is launched from England.

1920

1940

1980s

1977

The icebreaker *Artika* becomes the first nuclear powered ship that isn't a submarine to reach the North Pole.

1960

Container ships are commonly used to carry huge loads of cargo around the world.

1980

1997

The SB *Collinda* becomes the first solar powered boat to cross the English Channel.

2018

2000

The world's largest cruise ship sets sail from Barcelona, Spain.

2020

Glossary

cargo goods or things that are carried somewhere to be sold

engineer a person trained to design and build machines

hovercraft a vehicle that travels on a cushion of air

navy part of the armed services that works at sea

passenger someone other than the driver who rides in
a vehicle such as a boat or ship

refrigerated kept cold, for keeping food fresh

Find out more

Aircraft Carriers (Mighty MIlitary Machines), Matt Scheff (Raintree, 2018)

Big Machines Float!, Catherine Veitch (Raintree, 2015)

Boats (My First Discoveries), Christian Broutin (Moonlight Publishing, 2019)

Websites

www.scienceforkidsclub.com/boats.html
Discover fast facts about boats.

www.sciencekids.co.nz/sciencefacts/boats.html
Check out this website for fun facts about boats and ships

Index

Raintree is an imprint of Capstone Global Library Limited, a company incorporated in England and Wales having its registered office at 264 Banbury Road, Oxford, OX2 7DY – Registered company number: 6695582

www.raintree.co.uk
myorders@raintree.co.uk

Text © Capstone Global Library Limited 2020
The moral rights of the proprietor have been asserted.

Editor: Michelle Parkin
Designer: Rachel Tesch
Printed and bound in India

ISBN: 978 1 4747 6900 6 (hardback)   ISBN 978 1 4747 6904 4 (paperback)

British Library Cataloguing in Publication Data
A full catalogue record for this book is available from the British Library.

Acknowledgements
Alamy: Trinity Mirror/Mirrorpix, 30 (bottom left); Getty Images: Topical Press Agency/Stringer, 30 (top left), Universal History Archive, 30 (top right), Wild Horizon, 27; iStockphoto: AndyL, 24-25, BergmannD, 25 (inset), kentarus, 16-17, pidjoe, 7, spooh, 29, von Brandis, 4-5; Shutterstock: Alan Budman, 12, aragami12345s, 13, Dan Logan, 23, Dan Thornberg, cover (bottom middle), Darren Baker, 5 (inset bottom), EvrenKalinbacak, 22, Federico Rostagno, cover (bottom left), Flamingo Images, 28, FOTOGRIN, 26, freevideophotoagency, 5 (inset top), 10, GERARD BOTTINO, 30 (bottom right), Kanok Sulaiman, cover (bottom right), Macgork, 15, MKeerati, 18-19, Paul Vinten, cover (top), 1, Philip Bird LRPS CPAGB, 11, Rawpixel.com, 20-21, richardjohnson, 6, trek6500, 8-9, Yari Ghidone, 12, Yevgen Belich, 2-3